Direct Citizen Action

*****

How We Can Win the Second American Revolution Without Firing a Shot

By James Ostrowski

Cazenovia Books

Buffalo (USA)

PoliticalClassDismissed.com

FreetheChildren.US

D1502621

Published by Cazenovia Books, Buffalo, New York

Printed in the United States of America

ISBN13 978-0-9749253-4-9

First Edition

Library of Congress Control Number: (pending)

"What is of supreme importance in war is to attack the enemy's strategy."

—Sun Tzu

"A small body of determined spirits fired by an unquenchable faith in their mission can alter the course of history."

—Mohandas Gandhi

Contents

Preface

This is a book about strategy. Strategy has been a sorely neglected subject in the liberty movement. That is one of the reasons why the liberty movement has been so unsuccessful even though it is at least forty years old, has hundreds of thousands of committed activists and spends tens of millions of dollars each year. Hundreds if not thousands of people are employed in the liberty movement. If there is a single strategist so employed, it is one of the best kept secrets of all time.

Strategy can be a tricky word to precisely define. Let me propose a simple definition. *Strategy is your plan for victory!* Imagine a general with no plan for victory. He would be fired immediately. With no plan for victory, you are guaranteed to lose. You may have superb tactics and win many battles, as the American Army did in Vietnam; but without a strategy, those tactical successes do not serve the cause of ultimate victory.

The liberty movement has had no generally accepted and viable plan for victory. Thus it is no surprise that this movement has not only failed so far but liberty is shrinking each and every month at a seemingly accelerating pace. It is true that this cannot continue; that it will all implode at some point. This is not necessarily grounds for optimism, however. First, we don't know *when* it will implode and given the natural human lifespan of 80 years, wouldn't it be nice to know? Second, there is no guarantee that a libertarian society will emerge from the collapse of the American regime. The Soviet Union, for example, collapsed, yet this did not usher in a libertarian society in Russia. So, waiting around for the regime to collapse is not a plan for victory. It is the absence of a plan.

To have a strategy, a plan for victory, you need to be able to define what victory means. One of the many problems with the wars in Iraq and Afghanistan (and Vietnam) is lack of a clear definition of victory. That's why it was so galling when those of us who were against these wars were accused of opposing an American victory. How can we oppose something that was never defined?

One blogger wrote a so-called "strategy" for the tea party movement that was not a strategy at all but simply a set of policy proposals. That many people in the movement confuse goals with strategy is symptomatic of our plight.

Goal

↓

Strategy

↓

Tactics

↓

Execution

↓

Victory

I propose that our goal in the liberty movement should be restoring the old pre-Constitutional republic, the regime that the Minute Men and Washington's Army fought for and that Jefferson defined in 1776. We must move beyond the notion that praying to the Constitution will save us. If the purpose of the Constitution was to guarantee limited government, *it failed.* Face that sad fact and move on. Nostalgia is not a strategy.

This goal may seem radical to some and not radical enough for others. However, it is a reasonable compromise to hold all factions of the liberty movement together.

Restoring the old republic as a loose confederation of states would not be the end of history. Even better and bolder visions of individual liberty could still evolve within that flexible framework once the Leviathan in DC is finally overthrown.

Thus, without a goal, you can have no strategy. Once you have decided on a goal, you can then determine your strategy based on experience, research, and theory. Most discussions of strategy in the liberty movement have focused on education and political activity. Each has its place. However, as I argue in Chapter 3, politics is a rigged game so political activity is usually going to be a waste of scarce resources. Education is a critical and necessary element of any successful strategy. Yet, it is not a sufficient condition. The federal Leviathan needs a big push as well or it will not "go gentle into that good night." Only direct citizen action can provide that push.

****

This book presents both general strategic ideas and specific tactics. It is not by any means an exhaustive list. Rather, I hope that reading this book will get your own creative juices flowing. Americans excel at taking the initiative and improvising. American troops have done so many times in battle which is one reason they have prevailed against armies from authoritarian, hierarchical states. American citizens need to use that same native creativity and individual initiative in this battle for American freedom.

All I ask is that if you have discovered a great new tactic for direct action, please let me know about it so others around the country can quickly adopt your new idea in their own communities. Your ideas will be listed on the website, PoliticalClassDismissed.com/teaparty.

In addition to PCD, make a note to follow developments at FreetheChildren.US, the site devoted to my new book, *Government Schools Are Bad for Your Kids: What You Need to Know*.

Finally, for many of the tactics proposed in this book and for many to be rolled out in the near future, it is critical that we create the largest Twitter contact list in the country. Please register for updates at our account:

twitter.com/2dAmericanRev

Barack Obama has three million "followers." If the liberty movement can surpass that figure, the stage will be set for taking the concept of direct citizen action to a level never seen before!

Introduction

This book is for people who have concluded that America is in serious trouble because its government got too big. I make no effort to prove that here. I and many others have done that at length elsewhere. It is simply an assumption of the book. So, this is a book for libertarians, Paulians, tea party people, limited government conservatives and anyone else who accepts the above proposition. Let's call us *the liberty movement*.

Being a libertarian for thirty years, Ron Paul's election lawyer in New York State in 2007-8, and a leader of the tea party movement should give me the credibility to say what needs to be done now. I am not some Johnny-come-lately to the cause or a paid political hack for any party or plutocrat. I received no outside support to write or publish this book. I'm a working class lawyer who lives with his wife and two children in a three-bedroom home in a working class neighborhood in North Buffalo.

The impetus for this book was my fear that the liberty movement is being set up for a big disappointment in 2010 and 2012. While public opinion is turning our way and millions of grassroots activists hit the streets to protest big government last year, the odds are that the same GOP establishment whose free-spending ways and nation-building wars set the stage for Obama, will be choosing the candidates for Congress this year and will choose the nominee against Obama in 2012. These folks are unapologetic about their decades of support for big government policies, yet they will cleverly say the things their consultants tell them to say to appeal to the liberty movement.

There *will* be elation on election night this year, but then the sellouts will occur just as they did during the Reagan years, after the 1994 Republican "Revolution" and after the Republicans achieved total control of the federal government during the Bush years. I can see this happening because I have watched politics closely for many decades and I know how GOP operatives think and act.

Please understand that I do not oppose political activity altogether. Since I am a political consultant for liberty movement candidates, that would be economic suicide! My point is that electoral politics should be engaged in with great selectivity, only when the candidate is golden, such as Ron Paul, and other circumstances dictate that the scarce resources of the liberty movement can be applied to great effect in a key race.

Instead, our primary focus should be on the numerous and highly effective methods of direct citizen action that have been neglected by our movement but which have been highly effective in other times and places. Many of the ideas I propose here will also make electoral success for the liberty movement much more likely.

In the realm of politics, the best chance the liberty movement has is not winning elections but convincing states and localities to *stop cooperating with the federal government.* I believe the Tenth Amendment Movement as it is known has great potential. Early on, I criticized this movement for too much talk—meaningless resolutions—and not enough action such as telling the Feds where they can put all their money with anti-federal strings attached. Here's my post from March 10, 2009 on LewRockwell.com:

When words on paper have failed, add more words

That's how I see the state sovereignty resolutions, at least those I have read. This Arizona resolution urges the federal government to start respecting the Tenth Amendment. I have news for the drafters. They think they are respecting the Tenth Amendment. Here's what the resolution should have said if the supporters were really serious and not just chasing headlines or self-delusions. "All state legislation enacted under threat of the withdrawal of federal funds, and all state legislation that facilitates the administration of unconstitutional federal programs is hereby repealed."

I urge this movement to avoid direct confrontations with the Feds and instead use a more Zen-like approach: non-cooperation in all discretionary matters.[1] For example, while the Feds, with the blessing of our post-New Deal rubber-stamp Supreme Court, can apparently enact any drug laws it so chooses, I am not aware of any legal obligation that states and localities have to waste their scarce resources on the Feds' stupid drug war. The best way to

---

[1] I hinted at such a strategy in my 1998 article on secession. "Was the Union Army's Invasion of the Confederate States a Lawful Act?" in *Secession, State & Liberty*, David Gordon, ed., (New Brunswick, NJ: Transaction Publishers, 1998).

end the drug war is not through lobbying Congress but by persuading key cities to stop wasting their scarce resources on a destructive and unwinnable war.

For the latest developments in the Tenth Amendment Movement, see Michael Boldin's great website, TenthAmendmentCenter.com.

I am keeping this book concise to keep the cost down and make it available to a large readership. Therefore, please refer to my websites, PoliticalClassDismissed.com and FreetheChildren.US for further information and updates on direct citizen action in these times.

Part I Where We Stand; Where We Need to Go

1. The Sad State of the Nation

Barack Obama is not the problem with America. He is merely the symptom. When big government failed, the people, not knowing what went wrong, went for the fresh face who promised that government would solve the problems the people didn't know government caused in the first place.

America went off course many, many decades ago. Blaming Obama for our problems is like saying a 500-pound man is fat because he just ate three pizzas. Obama *is* the captain of the Titanic and his ship *is* speeding recklessly along, but he did not design the ship or place that giant iceberg in its path.

The tragedy is that the American people do not know why the economy collapsed. They do not know the nature of the regime that runs the country. They do not know that this regime is *not* the regime for which the Founding Fathers and Mothers fought. They do not know what the regime *was* that the Founders fought for. Finally, they do not know that the solution to our economic collapse is to restore that regime.

What *were* those Minute Men fighting for at Lexington and Concord? A republic of largely independent states. They weren't fighting for the Constitution. *There was no Constitution.* They were fighting for a republic that would protect their *natural right to liberty.*

What is a republic? There's much confusion about that. We must get this right. John Adams once complained that he "never understood" what the guarantee of republican government meant "and I believe no man ever did or will." With apologies to John Adams, by "republican," I mean a government exercising limited powers delegated to it by the people, whose officials are answerable to the people in regular, free elections.

Distinguishing between a republic and a democracy is critical. Both forms of government feature *voting by the people* to select officials. The difference between them is that while republican voting is done for the purpose of choosing officials to administer the government in the pursuit of its narrowly defined functions, democratic voting is done, not only to select officials but also to determine the functions and goals and powers of the government. The guiding principle of republics is that they exercise narrow powers delegated to them by the people, who themselves, as individuals, *possess such powers.* They cannot spring as they do in democracies, *ex nihilo,* from the mob's collective whim.

Only a republican government can be truly limited. A republican government may only exercise powers delegated by the people *that the people actually possess.* The people do not have the right to steal from their neighbors so they cannot delegate to the government the power to create a welfare state. The people do not have the right to counterfeit so they cannot delegate that power to the Federal Reserve. The people do not have the right to rule the world so they cannot delegate to the government the right to create a global military empire. You see where I am going with this? **If we had a republic, we would not be in the bloody mess we are in.**

In a democracy, there are no real limits to government power. If you object, you will always be told, hey, majority rules.

Long before Barack Obama was born, America traded in its decentralized libertarian republic for a centralized, democratic, corporate state with a global military empire.

You cannot destroy a great country immediately. By the 1970's, however, the corporate state, the welfare-warfare state started to cause economic stagnation and an endless series of domestic and foreign crises. Middle class living standards have been frozen in place for decades. Our standard of living was only maintained by smoke and mirrors: young mothers joining the workforce, parents working two or three jobs, credit card and mortgage debt, huge federal deficits, inflation and foreign borrowing. What is happening now is *judgment day*, the day of reckoning, the day the national Ponzi scheme collapsed. To con the people into thinking that all was well, our puppet masters created a lot of phony money and the bill is now due.

2. The Changes We Need

The solution to all this is quite simple. Here is what we need to do.

- Liquidate the global military empire, ending the two Asian land wars that George Bush got us into and the congressional Democrats and Obama helped pay for.

- Take the savings, trillions, and start liquidating the federal welfare state, buying out all Social Security recipients with lump sum payments.

- Abolish all the unconstitutional federal agencies and programs such as Education, Energy, HUD, HHS, and Agriculture.

- Then we can repeal the Income Tax Amendment, one of the worst things that ever happened to this country, except for possibly--

- The Federal Reserve–abolish it. Repeal the legal tender laws and gold and silver will automatically become market money.

- Now, add a couple of amendments to bring the moribund Constitution back to life. Ban all corporate welfare so we never again have bankster heists and corporate bailouts. And, since true federalism was destroyed in the Civil War, let's recognize what the Founders understood in 1776, that any republic has the right to withdraw from a union when it so chooses. That will guarantee that the federal government will never again turn into a monstrous, murderous, counterfeiting kleptocracy.

That was easy, but if that platform was put up to a vote, it would lose, big-time. So our real problem is how to put this plan into effect, how to restore the Republic, in short, how to win the Second American Revolution without firing a shot.

History—Pickett's Charge; the Charge of the Light Brigade—shows what happens when a smaller army attacks a larger army in a heavily fortified position. *They lose!*

The sad truth is, though we want to restore the spirit of the American Revolution, we are outnumbered by Redcoats! Redcoat is an apt term for our adversaries given their affinity for red ink, red ideas such as Marx's support for "free education for all children in public schools" and red blood spilled in Asian land wars.

The majority of Americans now support Redcoat government: an arrogant King in a big castle, with a large court, ruling by edict from a distant capital, endless wars across the ocean for a global empire, and heavy taxes to pay for those wars. And we are now embroiled in two land wars in Asia in countries that previously expelled *the British*! That's why Rudyard Kipling wrote:

When you're wounded and left on Afghanistan's plains,
And the women come out to cut up what remains,
Jest roll to your rifle and blow out your brains
An' go to your Gawd like a soldier.
Go, go, go like a soldier,
So-oldier of the Queen!

Maybe the Loyalists who fled to Canada should come back home. After all, the British ultimately won the Revolutionary War. *Their ideas prevailed.* The Revolution is dead—unless the liberty movement can revive it.

Let's assume for the sake of argument that about ten percent of Americans are fed up and ready for radical change. That means that 90% are not. That is a huge problem. Remember that at Lexington, when the government gun controllers and tax collectors came up the road, the men of the town greeted them with muskets ready to fire. Today, if we did that, most of the men of the town would side with the federales.

Ladies and gentlemen, we are in 1770 again, when there were a small number of radicals who wanted independence but most people wanted to stay with England.

Being outnumbered doesn't mean we can't win. History also teaches that a smaller, more dedicated army, with a just cause, can prevail against a larger, mercenary force. But we need to become more dedicated, more committed, and at the end of the day, we need to get larger. We need converts just as the Patriots did.

3. Why Politics Is Not the Answer

"He will win who knows when to fight and
when not to fight."

—Sun Tzu

There are three basic approaches to changing public
policy: politics (elections and lobbying), direct citizen action
and violence. We can quickly rule out violence as morally
repugnant, inefficient and unpredictable.

*Political action has rarely in human history caused government to
shrink in size and power.* The natural tendency of government
is to grow and expand its powers. The events of 2008-2010
illustrate that. Over time, it will tend to tax and spend
more, hire more people and assume more power over our
lives, liberty and property. Government policies change
continually but if you look closely, it is almost always in the
direction of bigger government. If you favor bigger
government, you really don't have to do anything. Just sit
back and enjoy the show. By the natural laws of politics,
governments will tend to grow. If you check back in five
years, it is highly likely that the government will be bigger
and more powerful. Government in America has grown
enormously since about 1917, the start of American
involvement in World War I. No coincidence there; war
grows the state.[2]

---

[2] See, Robert Higgs, *Crisis in Leviathan: Critical Episodes in the
Growth of American Government* (Oxford University Press, 1989).

12

By its nature, the state is the means by which some people can impose the costs of achieving their goals onto unwilling others. As Frederic Bastiat put it, "Government is the great fiction, through which everybody endeavors to live at the expense of everybody else." The desire to impose costs on others is virtually limitless. Thus, governments tend to grow over time.

There are five main reasons for this which are, unfortunately, structural features of political life:

1. *rational apathy*—the incentive some people have to increase the size of the state outweighs the incentive the rest of us have to fight them;

2. *government control over political ideas*— the state uses its control over schools and other idea-disseminating institutions to propagate support for further government growth;

3. *government creates its own demand*— because the state's various interventions into the market economy always fail (e.g., health care), ironically, they *increase* the demand of the uninformed majority for even further interventions to fix the problems caused by the prior interventions;

4. *the productivity of the mixed economy*— given the inherent tendency of the state to grow, only extreme dissatisfaction among the populace will rouse them to act; however, even a partially free market produces enough wealth to mollify the people;

5.   *government has a monopoly on the use of legal force*—government grows because it can. Given the universal human desire to accomplish goals with the least possible exertion, politicians have an irresistible urge to use the state's powers to continually expand the amount of wealth they control. Anyone who objects can always appeal to the politicians' judges and can expect to be told, "Get lost!"

Since it is in the structural DNA of government to grow, it is nearly impossible to persuade its officials to reverse that tendency or to persuade the voters to elect candidates who intend to shrink government. The last time a mass political movement was able to achieve power and shrink government was Thomas Jefferson's velvet Revolution of <u>1800!</u>

Ron Paul's campaign for president in 2007-8 showed how difficult it is to elect a candidate who favors smaller government. In spite of over 100,000 campaign workers and $30,000,000 and an articulate candidate with 20 years in Congress and a sterling personal life and record of accomplishment, he received less than ten percent in every Republican primary election. The system is thoroughly stacked against anyone who would attempt to reform it from within.

The main function of national elections in this country is to give the people the illusion that they are in charge and can change policy whenever necessary. However, the basic policies never seem to change. Elections allow people to blow off steam and thus serve as a safety valve for the regime that allows them to rule us for another four years.

With respect to the upcoming congressional elections this year, a Patriot candidate would need as much as two million dollars to run a competitive race for the House. Very few have that kind of money or can raise it. More likely, the Republican challengers this year will be party loyalists funded and controlled by the plutocrats and GOP establishment.

I know these are harsh realities to accept. They contradict what we have been taught in school and told to believe in endless TV ads urging us to vote and participate in the political process. However, to win this fight, you will have to be as clear-eyed as our adversaries are about the realities of power politics. That's how the political class got all that power in the first place: by seeing things clearly and not being fooled by myths and clichés.

4. Direct Action Works

"So in war, the way is to avoid what is strong and to strike at what is weak."

--Sun Tzu

Forget what they told you in high school civics class. Politics is rigged and voting is like trying to stop a hurricane with your breath. In sharp contrast, direct citizen action works. Gandhi used it to overthrow the British Empire. Martin Luther King used it to overthrow Jim Crow. The Patriots used it at the Boston Tea Party that sparked the American Revolution. Several velvet revolutions used direct action to overthrow communist regimes in Europe.

Why does direct action work while political action usually fails? Political action involves an effort to *change somebody else's mind about politics.* To engage in direct action, you do not need to change anyone's mind. Rather, you simply start doing things in your daily life that will move the country towards liberty, and stop doing things that hurt the cause of liberty.

Let's use as an example the most critical form of direct action you can take, pulling your kids out of government schools (see Chapter 11). Political action has failed to achieve real school choice or better schools. So, I have proposed a massive simultaneous withdrawal of children from the government schools. Each child removed is one fewer child indoctrinated to love big government and is one fewer child exposed to crime, drugs and promiscuity in government schools. You don't need anyone's permission to do this. Just do it!

16

Another example is proposed in Chapter 9: voting with your dollars. You can complain about politicians being bought off by big business. That is a waste of time. Or, you can boycott the firms that bankroll the politicians. Regardless of what others do, you will have thereby deprived the politicians of a small source of their revenue.

Bottom line. Politics is rigged but direct action works.

Part II How to Get There

5. It's Yours If You Want it[3]

Decide that you have had enough. You want to do something to reverse America's economic collapse. That something is nothing less than restoring the American republic. America's problems of today were caused by the abandonment of that Republic slowly over a long period of time. *Pledge allegiance to the principles of the American Revolution.*

This chapter might seem obvious or even unimportant. However, I want to emphasize that this is the most important chapter in the book. Why? Because most of the power of the government comes from the public perception that it is legitimate. For this insight, I am indebted to Étienne de la Boétie's *The Politics of Obedience: The Discourse of Voluntary Servitude* (1553) and his foremost modern exponent, Murray N. Rothbard.[4]

How do 545 people—a president, 535 congressmen and nine judges control a nation of over 300 million people? Certainly not by physical force. Could 545 gangsters gain control of the country by suddenly announcing that they are the legitimate government deserving of your allegiance? Obviously not because you would not choose to grant them power over you. This example shows that the source of federal power—not right but power—is the people's own "consent" to be governed. The American people hold the keys to their own jail cells between their ears and can leave

---

[3] A favorite exhortation of legendary cross-country coach Bob Ivory.
[4] Rothbard's introduction to the 1975 edition is online at http://mises.org/rothbard/boetie.asp.

the prison of tyranny any time a sufficient number of them choose to be free.

So, the first thing you have to do is withdraw that "consent" and make that known whenever possible.[5] History shows that regimes fall when the masses withdraw their "consent." I am not urging you to do anything illegal or violent, just come to the realization that you will no longer give *any* moral sanction or support to the corrupt kleptocracy on the Potomac. A journey of 1000 miles begins with a single step. This is the critical first step from which all else follows.

You need to withdraw your support for the corrupt regime the federal government has become. That is easy. *Just stop.* Stop voting for those degenerates and don't vote for their opponents either unless they are Patriots. Stop being silent when people talk about politics. State your opinion clearly. Tell people you've joined the Second American Revolution and urge them to do so as well.

****

Permit me to digress into a discussion of the meaning of political consent and its withdrawal. I am not saying that the American people ever explicitly consented to be ruled by the regime on the Potomac, or that they are parties to some mysterious Social Contract that implies their consent. That is all utter nonsense and propaganda. I know I never consented to be ruled by a regime that I have strongly opposed since my teenage years. Nor have I ever signed a Social Contract allowing them to rule over me. I'd be a jackass if I had.

---

[5] This is precisely what Murray Rothbard proposes in his introduction to *The Politics of Obedience.*

To the best of my knowledge, no living American ever signed a contract to be ruled by the creepy politicians in DC. There are people long dead who signed a proposed Constitution and there are 1179[6] people long dead who voted at state conventions to ratify the Constitution. However, no living American ever agreed to be bound by the consent to be governed apparently given by people long dead that they did not know.

Libertarian legal scholar Randy Barnett has brilliantly refuted all possible theories of how citizens can be found to have *implicitly* consented to be ruled when it is perfectly obvious that they have not *explicitly* consented. See, *Restoring the Lost Constitution* (2004), pp. 11 et seq.

Voting does not imply consent as we never get to vote on the legitimacy of the regime itself. And what if you vote *against* the regime as I have done in every election since I was allowed to vote? How in the world can that be construed as consent? Well, I played the game. Okay, so if I stop voting, I have withdrawn my consent? That's a bargain! I will stop voting, withdraw my consent and the tax bills will cease. Hurray! Yeah, but you *could have* played the game, they will say. Barnett replies: "It is a queer kind of 'consent' where there is no way to refuse one's consent." (p. 16). Barnett goes on to demolish all the familiar rationalizations for why average citizens have "consented" to be governed by political thugs in DC:

1. *Residency*—this argument "presupposes that those who demand that you leave already have authority over you." (p. 18) It's a circular argument.
2. *Acquiescence to the laws.* "Does one really manifest a consent to obey the commands of

---

[6] In 14 states including Vermont.

someone much more powerful simply because one does not physically resist the threat of violence for noncompliance?" (p. 21)

3. *Acceptance of the regime.* This proves too much, according to Barnett. Even oppressive regimes have the passive acceptance of their people in the sense they do not actively revolt.

4. *Acceptance of benefits.* This is the most common argument made by liberals these days. With respect to the alleged benefits of the state's legal system, Barnett simply notes that there can be no consent since there is no way to opt out. The argument from receipt of tangible "benefits" also fails. These are paid for by compulsory taxes you never consented to. Only if such things as roads, schools, and fire protection were funded voluntarily, could you be said to have consented to the regime by using them. That never happened of course. Also, again, to consent, there must be a reasonable way not to consent. If I refuse to use the streets, I die of starvation. It's a distorted view of consent that leads to the "argument": join us or die!

Thus, we the living never consented to the current regime in the first place in any meaningful way. Thus, what I am proposing is this: we need to make explicit what is already implicit. We need to announce that we do not accept the legitimacy of the regime. This regime is blatantly, openly and proudly violating our natural rights. It is not legitimate within the clear understanding of our founding document, the Declaration of Independence. Thus, you have no moral obligation to support it. Withdrawing moral support for the regime is critical since public support is the very basis of the regime's power. That is why government schools are so critical to the maintenance of the regime's power. And that is why even totalitarian regimes have elaborate propaganda operations.

I emphasize again that I do not advocate civil disobedience. Why engage in risky and costly law-breaking when we can take America back through lawful and peaceful means?

If *the regime* begins to unambiguously violate its own constitution, then *it becomes the practitioner of civil disobedience* and the people will have a moral and legal right to resist as I explain further in Chapter 20.

6. Education

Our next task is obvious: education. We need to educate ourselves before we can educate others. We need to study the history and principles of the American Revolution. We need to study war and peace. *War is the health of the state.* We need to study economics.

Let's take a quick look at the American Revolution.

- England needed money *for war.*
- They taxed the Colonists.
- The Colonists didn't want to pay.
- England sent troops and tax collectors armed with general warrants to find taxable stuff.
- The Colonists got angry and threatened resistance.
- The English decided to seize the Colonists' guns.
- War broke out.

Lessons:

- War means high taxes.
- Taxes mean invasion of privacy.
- To steal your money and violate your privacy, the government must disarm you first.
- You have the natural right to resist tyranny.
- Gun control was the proximate cause of the American Revolution.
- America was born in an act of resistance to gun control!

Economics. If the American people understood one simple principle, we could shrink the size of government by 90% in three months. What principle? *All resources are scarce.* If we could only understand that principle, which just happens to be the first law of economics, then all the politicians' lies about adding new programs like the bailout and stimulus would be laughed at.

So, we need to teach ourselves economics at home school—the living room laptop or the desk top computer in the basement. What does the free market have to do with the Republic? Everything! Republican government exists to protect private property. The free market is the free exchange of private property. A true republic can only have a free market economy.

In 2006, I prepared a short study guide to basic economics for Free New York, Inc. That paper is republished here at Appendix "B". My goal was to present citizens with enough information so they can easily see that almost everything they hear from politicians about economics is dishonest nonsense.

Why can't a republic have a global military empire? An empire is designed to rule other nations for their benefit or ours. If it's the former, it violates the purpose of a republic as limited to protecting the rights of its own citizens, not the planet's. If it's the latter, then the republic violates its own premise, the natural rights of all human beings. Empires require huge armies and bureaucracies and oppressive taxes that violate our right to private property, the right to keep what we earn. Empires, as Washington taught us, invite retaliation and thus the government betrays its only true purpose by jeopardizing the lives and security of its citizens by pointlessly manufacturing foreign enemies.

Through education, you can immunize yourself from the lies of politicians. If any politician tells you they will improve your life, they are lying. Do not believe them.

How do you know a politician is lying? Their lips are moving. Teach your children not to believe them either. A politician will tell you face to face he will do this or that for you, then, as soon as you turn your back on him, he will pick your pocket to pay for the same promise he made to your neighbor.

Tolstoy wrote the politician's credo:

"I sit on a man's back, choking him and making him carry me, and yet assure myself and others that I am very sorry for him and wish to ease his lot by all possible means— except by getting off his back."

The Mises Institute has created the best site on the web for people to educate themselves about economics, history and politics. I have started to gather the very best of their materials, especially audio and video programs at PolticalClassDismissed.com/teaparty. I recommend that you start with Professor Ralph Raico's superb series, *History: The Struggle for Liberty*. Then, dig into the lectures by the Mises Institute's incomparable team of scholars who are able to speak plain English while maintaining the highest standards of their respective fields.

7. Recruitment

Let's not confuse majority opposition to Obama and the Democrats with solid support for restoring the old Republic. Most people are not there yet. We need more Patriots, fast.

There is no easy way to do this. To use football coach Woody Hayes's motto: "Three yards and a cloud of dust." We need to run the ball right up the middle.

Once you understand America's history, the dynamics of war and peace and the principles of market economics (See Appendix "B"), start making more Patriots. Begin with your family and friends, then co-workers, customers, clients, neighbors and members of your church or your gym if fitness is your religion.

Make a list of the people you know and who respect your opinion. Write them a letter and tell them you have joined a movement to restore the American Republic and save the nation from the Redcoats who have destroyed it. Invite them to do the same. Host a meeting at your home to discuss the matter further. Create an email list of those who are interested in the liberty movement.

Send them a link to the resource page at PoliticalClassDismissed.com/teaparty. Finally, ask them to register at Twitter.com/2dAmericanRev to receive news about direct action activities.

8. Rescuing Patriotism

We need to get people's attention. We need a new symbol of patriotism because the current symbols of patriotism have lost their meaning. What does the current flag stand for? Limited government? A true republic? Minding our own business in the world as Washington advised? Obviously not. In fact, the flag is used to glorify a regime that would make the Patriots sick to their stomachs.

So I proposed in April of 2009 that we use the Betsy Ross flag to symbolize *our* movement. Our adversaries have their symbols; we will have better ones. This idea has already gained supporters as almost any large tea party rally shows.

There is a great symbol out there for the taking that is universally understood to stand for the old republic. I propose we bring it to life again as the symbol of our movement and, further, to use it as a *battle* flag. Battle flags serve the critical function of identifying allies during the chaos of battle. When we see that flag, wherever we are in the country, we will know there is a kindred spirit behind that door.

As this movement grows, these flags will start dominating the landscape and we will know that victory is near.

9. Vote With Your Dollars

We need to think about the things we do every day and figure out how we can integrate the liberty movement into those daily routines. One thing we do every day is spend money. We buy things. We buy services. We pay bills.

How do politicians win elections? By buying TV time. Where do they get the money? Much of it comes from private businesses or private persons who run or own business firms. We know who they are and so I say to you: stop slitting your own throats. *Stop buying things from business firms that fund the political machine and fund the corporate state and fund big government.*

You can go down to Congressman Smith's office and talk to his staff till you are blue in the face about getting rid of the Federal Reserve. They *will* ignore you and when you leave they will have a good laugh at your expense. Or, you can stop giving your money to his bankrollers. One tactic is a complete waste of time. The other will hurt his ability to raise money. If he can't raise money, we can beat him when our numbers grow.

Boycott the bankers of the political class. Starve the Redcoats and Loyalists!

Now, if you are boycotting those fat cats and their firms, you are going to have to spend your money elsewhere. Here too you can directly aid the liberty movement with each purchase. If we have ten percent of the population on our side, we probably have *twenty-five percent* of small businesses. Small business owners are natural libertarians. You do not have to tell them that taxes are oppressive and government regulations can strangle them. They know it because they live that nightmare each day. So I say, buy from Patriots. They will return the favor later in too many ways to imagine now. To hell with Redcoat companies. In this country, money talks. In politics, it is the only thing that does.

You want to win this fight? You want a free country? *Buy it!*

How do we know which businesses to patronize? Easy. Look for the Betsy Ross flag, the flag the Patriots flew.

PoliticalClassDismissed.com/teaparty will have the links you need to check on those in your area who are bankrolling the politicians.

For many years, I have urged small business people to lead the fight for liberty in Western New York. I gave this speech in Buffalo in 2005:

> *"The only hope for Western New York is for the independent business class to slough off their normal and understandable political apathy; take charge and lead a populist revolt of the outsiders against the insiders."*

> Why small business? Who else feels the full effects of taxes and regulations? Government employees? Obviously not. Employees of any kind? No. They don't feel the full impact of income taxes because, by virtue of the magic of withholding, they never had that money in their pockets in the first place. It is as though it never existed. If their job consists of complying with government regulations, then that is their livelihood. But if you are an *owner*, you have to write those checks to the taxman and you know that every dollar you spend complying with government regulations is a dollar that comes out of your profits.

> What about big business? Why are they hopeless? Merely because it is their system

we are living under. It's their system we are fighting. We have met the enemy and it is the alliance of big government and big business. If I am wrong, please tell me why there are no corporate fat cats here today. Why do they do so little to change things around here? Because they like the way things are. Where else can fifty guys call the shots in a large metropolitan area: pick the mayor, the county executive, *the judges, the prosecutors*. Life is good!

But what about all those high taxes and suffocating regulations? Don't they hurt big business also? Not quite. First, big business uses corporate welfare to get special tax breaks and regulatory leniency. Warren Buffett was able to get a special exemption for GEICO employees who are selling car insurance. Second, it is not a level playing field. Regulations favor larger firms which can spread the costs around better. Further, many big businesses are joined at the hip with the government: the banks who get to borrow the Fed's freshly printed money at rates denied to regular folk; the defense contractors; and all the hospitals and the Buffalo Medical Campus which are mostly funded by the government.

So, *you are our only hope*. You have many advantages in this battle. You have some spare change. You have brains, a work ethic and organizational skills. You are leaders. You have the respect of your communities, families and friends. You are independent. The powers that be cannot fire you for taking a stand.

And you are going to need all those
resources and more and some luck. You are
up against a ruthless, entrenched multi-
billion dollar political machine with
thousands of soldiers whose jobs depend on
beating you. Don't have any illusions about
going into this battle. Just think of Pickett's
Charge but imagine a different outcome."

One particular type of business, restaurants and
taverns, could be particularly useful in this cause. No
industry suffers more from big government than restaurants
and taverns. Their owners and employees work their hearts
out for the privilege of paying high taxes. In some areas like
Western New York, the property and sales taxes are
confiscatory. And those taxes come out of their bottom
line. Only a silly economist who never ran a business would
say that you merely "pass them along" to your customers.
At the end of the year, much of what they have left is
shipped off to the state capital or Washington DC to be
spent by hack politicians who wouldn't know you if they fell
on top of you.

It is time for restaurant and tavern owners to get
politically active. This would be merely reviving an old
American tradition. During the first Revolution, taverns
were vital meeting places for the Revolutionaries and served
as the nerve centers of the revolt. Here's an excerpt from a
webpage[7] honoring the '76 House in Tappan, New York:

"Daniel Webster called America's
colonial taverns 'The headquarters of the
Revolution.' Patrons of this tavern knew it
as 'The listening post of the Revolution';

---

[7] http://www.76house.com/history_role.html

they knew that Washington made his headquarters at that building of like vintage just across the creek.

"Sam Adams plotted that timely Tea Party at Boston's *Green Dragon Tavern.* Thomas Jefferson drafted elements of the Declaration of Independence at a tavern, the *Indian Queen* in Philadelphia. Patrick Henry and Virginia's restless patriots pledged their lives to liberty or death at the *Raleigh Tavern* in Williamsburg, the first building of that colonial town's restoration.

"Across the colonies, taverns were where town folk and country folk kept in touch, one with another, where they got the news and the gossip."

I intend to contact the restaurant and tavern owners in my community and ask them to get involved in this cause. I urge you to do the same. They can supply free meeting places for your local movements in exchange for the much-needed business your group can supply. It's a win-win arrangement.

Small and family-owned and independent businesses have been generally absent in politics. That's understandable. They have been busy making a living. But they can no longer ignore the decline of their nation and the economy upon which their very survival depends. Join us before it is too late. Post the Betsy Ross flag on your front door and watch the Patriots stream in, hungry and thirsty from boycotting Redcoat establishments just as their forefathers did.

10.   Vote With Your Feet

If you live in a state that lacks the freedom you need to pursue the American Dream, it may be time to *vote with your feet* and, in effect, cast the deciding vote for lower taxes and more liberty.   Scholars Jason Sorens and William P. Ruger have performed a valuable service by ranking the fifty states by how much personal and economic freedom they allow their citizens.[8]   The degree of freedom in education is heavily weighted in the study: "The reason we consider education regulations so critically important is that they affect the future course of liberty by affecting how and what the next generation is taught." Here are the winners:

Overall Freedom Ranking

1. New Hampshire 0.432
2. Colorado 0.421
3. South Dakota 0.392
4. Idaho 0.356
5. Texas 0.346
6. Missouri 0.320
7. Tennessee 0.284
8. Arizona 0.279
9. Virginia 0.275
10. North Dakota 0.268

---

[8] Freedom in the Fifty States: An Index of Personal and Economic Freedom (Mercatus Center, George Mason University, Feb. 2009).

Listed below are the ten *least free states*, states that tend to take your spare change in taxes and also allow less choice in K-12 education. The authors single out Hawaii, Washington State, and oddly enough, Tennessee, the seventh freest state, for having burdensome education regulations. Idaho and Indiana on the other hand allow much educational freedom.

41. Connecticut -0.225
42. Illinois -0.238
43. Massachusetts -0.242
44. Washington -0.275
45. Hawaii -0.304
46. Maryland -0.405
47. California -0.413
48. Rhode Island -0.430
49. New Jersey -0.457
50. New York -0.784

Jason Sorens helped found the Free State Project which seeks to persuade 20,000 citizens to move to New Hampshire and make it even freer than it is today. Their website is at FreeStateProject.org. All I can say is, what a great idea!

A less drastic option is moving to another county which could merely involve a move of a few miles. The Tax Foundation publishes a valuable report each year listing each county's property taxes. Even counties in high property tax states such as New York can vary widely in the level of property taxes. For example, the median property tax in Monroe County (Rochester), New York was $3,705 in 2008 but was only $3052 in neighboring Ontario County. The bottom line is, whether or not you are considering moving or buying your first home, think hard before moving into a high tax town, school district, county or state. By avoiding those places, you will not only save extra dollars but you will also send a badly needed message of change to high tax regimes.

Every time you take an action that reduces government spending you perform the critical task of starving the beast! Total government spending is about $6,400,000,000,000 each year. Let's assume for the sake of argument that the forces of big government directly spend one percent of their receipts or $64,000,000,000 each year maintaining and expanding their power. (That's probably an understatement.) That sum is derived, directly or indirectly from total spending. For example, a corporation that kicks back donations to politicians who secured a grant for the corporation, is clearly recycling the grant money for political contributions. Thus, we can derive this rule of thumb: every hundred dollars of government spending generates a dollar that is used to maintain the status quo.

So in the example above, each family moving out of overtaxed Monroe County deprives "the machine" of $6.50 they could spend on donations, lobbying and government propaganda such as government school "history" classes. That may seem like a trivial amount, but it's not. If we can multiply that savings by millions of other Patriots making similar decisions on every level of government, we will have starved the beast of billions of dollars!

Now, look at the other side of the equation. How much money does the Liberty Movement spend each year? I alluded to this in the Preface. My estimate is about one hundred million each year. Let's compare what "we" spend to what "they" spend. The difference is astounding. We are outspent 640 to one! So, don't dismiss small acts of starving the beast of a mere ten dollars when we only have one cent to match it.

To starve the beast, follow the strategies and tactics set forth in Chapters 9, 10, 11 and 14.

11. Pull Your Kids Out of Government Schools

This is the most important action you can take to save America, not to mention your own kids. I recently wrote a book about it and can only summarize it here. See, *Government Schools Are Bad for Your Kids: What You Need to Know* (Nov. 2009). The website for the book is FreetheChildren.US.

Government schools were not established out of any dire need for them but rather for a variety of crass religious, political and economic motives. They were not immaculately conceived but rather were born out of a toxic stew of religious absolutism, Prussian militarism, utopian socialist leveling, special interest greed and power lust.

Today, government schools are loaded with crime, bullying, drugs and sexual promiscuity. They indoctrinate students into a false view of American history, one that is invariably favorable to ever-expanding government.

It is a myth that parents can escape to the suburbs to avoid exposing their children to school crime. A study by the Manhattan Institute found virtually equal rates of delinquency in suburban schools. Government schools are unresponsive, self-serving bureaucracies that have to take eligible students even with criminal records, assuming they even know they have criminal records! They may even *want* to accept such students because they mean more state aid. Crime in government schools is in the nature of things. You get what you pay for.

Open and notorious and explicit sexual activity has also become a feature of daily life in government schools. Many government schools are turning into fornicatoriums featuring more and more sex, and less and less education.

Moving on to drugs, your local government high school is often the best drug store in town. One *suburban* high school in Upstate New York is nicknamed "Heroin High." Government schools are the key distribution point for illegal drugs in many communities. One study concluded that "80% of the nation's high school students and 44% of middle-schoolers have personally seen illegal drugs used or sold and/or students drunk or high on the grounds of their schools."[9] Another study warns that rates of illegal drug use are no lower in suburban schools.[10]

Why is the problem so bad? Government schools are filled with people who don't want to be there and who are bored and alienated. As we are constantly reminded by those who defend government schools: *they must take all students*. The fact that your kids spend six hours a day with fellow students subject to virtually no screening process is hardly a recommendation. It is also difficult to discipline students. So doing involves a whole host of legal and bureaucratic procedures. In private schools, disruptive students can easily be expelled. In government schools, those in charge of student discipline are bureaucrats, not particularly responsive to parental or student concerns. Private school principals must be responsive or face closing their doors due to a lack of customers.

A word to the wise should be sufficient. If you send your child to a government school, they may learn more about chemistry than you could possibly imagine.

---

9 Salynn Boyles, "Parents Blind to Rising School Drug Use", WebMD Medical News (Aug. 16, 2007).
10 J. P. Greene & G. Forster, *supra*.

Psychotropic drugs. As many as six percent of students in some government high schools are taking psychotropic drugs.[11] Psychotropic drugs are powerful, mind-altering chemicals that can cause serious temporary and permanent side-effects. They are often given to bored students whose behavior disrupts classrooms. They are a method of control in a regime premised on control. *The use of drugs to control students is the natural consequence of a system that forces parents to send their children to school and forces the children to be there.* That's all the law can accomplish: guaranteeing their physical presence. It cannot guarantee they will show up ready to learn or be docile. That's where the drugs—chemical coercion—come in.

Sentencing your children to thirteen years in government school subjects them to running a gauntlet of endless assaults on their well-being.

There is an epidemic of bullying in the government schools. It is commonplace to point out that many bullies are themselves victims of bullying who merely pass it along to those who are weaker since they can't strike back at the strong. The irony of the government school, *the biggest bully of young people in America,* urging its victims to stop being bullies is completely lost on the bureaucrats.

Government schools are glorified daytime prisons operating in an atmosphere of legally enforced nihilism which defaults into the pseudo-religion of hedonism. *The hedonistic atmosphere of government schools is a necessary reflection of the nature of those schools.* No reform is possible because such reform would make government schools the opposite of what they are: private schools.

There is only one way out: **out!**

---

[11] "U.S. Kids Take More Psychotropic Drugs Than Europeans," Health.com, Sept. 24, 2008.

In a republic, the theory is that power proceeds from the people and the government is the people's agent and servant. However, when the government, through its control of the schools, is given the power to shape the political mindset of its own citizens, that master-servant relationship is turned upside down. *The government becomes the master, the citizen the servant,* first inside the classroom but eventually outside it too.

In light of the obvious propaganda function of government schools, it must be emphasized that on a wide range of critical subjects, government schools would appear to be incapable of providing proper instruction at all! These include all the subjects where political philosophy plays an obvious role: history, civics, politics, law, ethics, and economics. Economist Ludwig von Mises believed it was "impossible to deal with any chapter of history without taking a definite stand on . . . implied economic doctrines."[12] He added, "The party that operates the schools is in a position to propagandize its tenets and to disparage those of other parties."[13]

Eventually, we come to the present sad state where the vast majority of the American people are unaware of their own true history. Being unaware, and thinking that the current regime is the best of all possible worlds, they are utterly unequipped to deal with the harsh new reality that the regime is failing and the nation is in the process of economic collapse.

What historical points of view have been suppressed, ignored or disparaged in the government schools?— Precisely those that would be extremely valuable to

---

[12] *Human Action: A Treatise on Economics* (Contemporary Books: Chicago, 3rd. Rev. ed., 1949) p. 877.
[13] *Id.*

Americans right now to help us navigate out of the mess we are in.

It is critical for American citizens to understand their own history. However, they get a skewed view of history when the government controls the schools. A proper study of history *must* include alternative views and not simply the views that happen to be favored by the regime that controls the schools. Students should be given unimpeded access to information on controversial aspects of history so they can learn how to think for themselves and reach their own conclusions.

Currently, America is in a state of crisis caused by its global military empire, gigantic welfare state and the business cycle caused by the Federal Reserve. (On that evil institution, see Ron Paul's bestseller, *End the Fed.*) Yet, Americans are handicapped in dealing with these crises because few Americans know that the Federal Reserve causes a boom and bust cycle and that 9/11 was blowback for decades of Federal intervention into the Middle East.[14] Thus, they fall for doomed policies such as Bush's War on Terror and Obama's bailout of the auto industry.

Worse yet, spending on government schools has established a permanent and large source of funding and workers for liberal Democratic causes. For example, Clarence, New York, is an affluent suburb outside of Buffalo where Republicans outnumber Democrats, 64 to 36 percent. However, the Clarence Teachers Association is an affiliate of the New York State United Teachers and the American Federation of Teachers, both of which heavily bankroll Democratic candidates. Money flows from the taxpayers to the school district to the teachers to the unions to the Democratic Party. Thus, Republican parents who

---

[14] See, Chalmers Johnson, "Blowback," *The Nation* (Sept. 27, 2001).

send their children to Clarence schools, are, in effect, bankrolling the treasury and ground troops of the party they vehemently oppose. To paraphrase Lenin, the capitalists are giving the socialists the rope they need to hang them.

America was supposed to be a highly decentralized peaceful commercial republic based on individual freedom and strictly limited government that minded its own business and stayed out of foreign conflicts. Instead, it is a highly centralized and militarized global empire whose extensive control over every aspect of our daily lives is rationalized by a distorted concept of majority rule that would have horrified the Founders—*that majorities have a right to destroy individual liberty.*

We have gone from a nation founded on loyalty to principles, including *the right of revolution against tyranny*, to one founded on loyalty to the government. Government schools are the foundation of big government in America.

The grand result of our experiment with government schools is a population ill-prepared to deal with the present crisis in America.

It is time to pull the plug while there is still a country worth saving.

12. Be a Knowledgeable Juror

Here's another form of direct citizen action you can take. The original Patriots did not trust government, including prosecutors or judges. They knew the only way to restrain the power of government was by *external* checks and balances. These include the right to bear arms and juries. Naturally, the government has tried to take both of these rights away from us. The right to bear arms is safe for the moment but let's talk about juries.

The original concept of a jury was that it could override the judge on matters of law. Call that jury nullification. Every prominent founder who was a lawyer stated explicitly that juries have the right to judge the law itself and whether it would be unjust to convict a defendant for violating that law under the circumstances.[15]

Tyrannical judges have ruled otherwise, thus overruling the Constitution by judicial fiat.

The bottom line is this. The Founders believed that juries have a constitutional right to judge the law in a criminal case and any judge who says otherwise hasn't studied our constitutional history.

The purpose of republican government is to protect the individual's right to life, liberty and property. The Founders created a jury system to ensure that no one was convicted of a crime unless they violated the life, liberty or property of a fellow citizen. If you get a jury notice, don't grumble. Show up and assert your rights and keep in mind

---

[15] J. Ostrowski, "The Rise and Fall of Jury Nullification," 15 *Journal of Libertarian Studies* 89 (Spring 2001).

that no one can tell you how to cast your vote in that jury room.

Now, just for the record, I'm not saying jurors should violate the law and lie to judges about their willingness to follow their instructions on the law. *What I'm saying is that judges should follow the law and should not lie to jurors!*

13. Ostracize Politicians

Politicians who refuse to change their ways even though there is overwhelming evidence they are destroying the country and imposing great harm on their own constituents and communities—should not be welcome in polite society. They should be ostracized and shunned. Instead, they are often treated like celebrities. This has to stop. Start treating them like the moral lepers they are.

Imagine a politician walking into the local diner. The owner comes up and says, "Joe, I don't know how to break this to you, but my customers don't want you in here. You will have to leave."

Wouldn't it be nice to see signs and bumper stickers pop up across America that say: **"Politician-Free Zone"**?

Don't be a sap and always fight your opponents with *their* weapons of choice and at the time and place of *their* choosing. Make these degenerate creeps fight on your own terms and on your own battlefield.

Surprise them! Revenge is a dish best served cold!

14. Minimize Your Contacts With Government

If you want smaller government, start acting like you mean it. Don't run off to this or that government agency whenever you have a problem. Start being self-reliant. Seek out private sector solutions to your problems. Whenever possible, avoid contacts with the government, especially the federal, state and county governments.

Here are some examples. The City of Buffalo recently started busing Catholic school students. My wife and I refuse to use the service. It's not the government's job to get my kids to school.

The courts are clogged with petty criminal and civil matters. If you have a minor dispute with someone, don't use the police and courts as a free payback service. Try to resolve your problems in another way. Use private mediators or arbitrators to resolve minor civil disputes or just offer to buy the other fellow a cup of coffee.

Don't buy lottery tickets. You are just giving the politicians more money to build their machines. You want to gamble? Buy stocks.

When you give charitable donations, reward organizations that refuse to take government money.

Granted, we are often forced to deal with the government. I am not asking you to be a hermit. All I am saying is, when you have an option, avoid the government. If you are going to talk limited government, start living it!

Part III How You Can Survive the Journey

While we are taking the country back, things may get worse before they get better. There may be civil unrest as the economy collapses. The government may use unrest as an excuse to grab dictatorial power. History tells us so. Governments have been known to use contrived energy and food shortages for political purposes such as discouraging resistance or buying off dissidents with promises of food and fuel.

In Part III, I present some practical advice on how to survive intact during these possible crises. Your motto should be: *hope for the best; prepare for the worst.*

15. Security

You are responsible for your family's basic security. In a crisis, there may be no time to call 911. In times of unrest, you may not have a working phone. If the government itself assumes dictatorial powers, the person on the other end of the 911 call will not be your friend.

Bottom line: you need to be armed.

If money is not an issue, you should have three weapons, a handgun, a shotgun and a rifle. Each has certain uses and advantages and disadvantages. LewRockwell.com has run a series of articles that explains which types of weapons you should acquire and how to use them. See PoliticalClassDismissed.com/teaparty for links to those articles.

If money is an issue, and you can only afford one weapon, get a shotgun. It's an ideal weapon to defend your home against intruders. If you have plenty of ammo and know what you're doing, you can hold off a hostile gang for a considerable period of time with one of those babies.

It is advisable to attend a firearms safety course and familiarize yourself with local, state and federal laws concerning firearms ownership.

Finally, do yourself a favor and install motion detector lights around the entire perimeter of your home.

16. Finances

I am not a financial planner or advisor so this chapter will be short.

America is drowning in debt, both private sector and public sector debt. Debt robs you of financial independence. You can't spend on your own priorities but must take care of your creditors. They own you. Also, debt makes you the possible plaything of politicians who may promise debt relief if you sell your political soul to them.

If you are in debt, you need to immediately cut back on spending and begin to pay it down. You may also have to increase your income if spending cuts don't do the trick.

These points may be obvious, but they still need to be stated.

All that said, the main point I need to emphasize here is you need to be prepared for a currency collapse, a hyperinflation where the fiat dollar becomes nearly worthless.

In times of unrest, fiat paper money tends to lose value and hard money becomes essential. Thus, you should begin acquiring at least small amounts of gold and silver. These will serve you well in a crisis. As the commercial says, gold has never been worth zero!

17. Feeding Your Family

I believe that each Patriot should be prepared to survive on his own for one year if all hell breaks loose in society. The key point is this: we have seen in history that during times of crisis, men and women with empty stomachs and hungry children have sold their souls to men on "white horses" such as Hitler and Stalin. They would later learn to regret it. So, this is a no-brainier. Remain self-sufficient so you won't have to make that choice.

That is not an insurmountable task. One website will sell you food for four for one year for about $2,700.[16] How you spend your money is up to you. Risk is a subjective calculation unique to each person. The point is, have an emergency food supply on hand for a duration that makes sense to you, based on your resources and sense of the future. Then, hope you never need it.

---

[16] SurvivalAcres.com.

18.   Heating Your Home

If the goal is to be able to survive one year of civil unrest, that means in most areas you need to be able to heat your home for about six months without relying on the utilities.

First of all, buy a generator. That will help if the utilities go dark but gasoline is still available. During times of unrest, however, gasoline itself tends to dry up.

Even without gasoline for a generator, you can still heat your home. If you have a fire place, it's a snap. Buy enough fire wood for the duration. If you have less, just use less and endure a lower average temperature. If you don't have a working fireplace, buy a wood-burning stove. They can heat your home quite nicely.

Beyond that, you have two other inexpensive options. Oil lamps offer many advantages, according to the blogger Judy of the Woods (judyofthewoods.net):

- "very cheap to run - can even burn used cooking oil
- the fumes are less toxic than those of paraffin candles or mineral oil lamps
- the production of renewable vegetable oil is less harmful to the environment than petroleum based products (including paraffin candles)
- for the extreme survivalist, vegetable oil is easier to store in bulk, or can even be produced on the home farm

- due to the wider base, more stable than candles, the flame of any burning wick falling into the oil will be extinguished
- odour free when using olive oil"

Candles are the final option. They are cheap and provide light and surprising amounts of heat. They can certainly keep the temperature above freezing in a small room. It beats the alternative. For about $25, you can buy the Kandle Heeter, a candle holder that concentrates the heat in a smaller area instead of upward and outward. Buy it at HeatStick.com.

19.   Emergency Communications

This will be short and sweet. If the power grid goes out and the internet is shut off, how do you find out what the hell is going on? There are basically two answers: shortwave radio and citizens band radio. Neither is particularly expensive. A CB costs about $50. A shortwave is a bit more. If you can't afford both, get a CB radio. With that, you will have access to information from short wave radio through third parties. If you can't afford either one, make sure you know a family member or friend who does and is close by.

20.   Be Prepared to Form a Neighborhood Militia

This book calls for peaceful, legal, direct citizen action to restore the old republic and our natural right to liberty. Patriots should not use violence or break the law to achieve their goals. We are the men and women of peace since *peace is simply another word for liberty*! Our opponents are the thugs.

Yet, liberty implies the right to defend yourself against tyranny. Thankfully, that right is built into the Constitution itself at the Second Amendment.

The liberal media has of course distorted the concept of a militia. It's not vigilante justice or a gang of terrorists or racists. No, the militia in a republic is simply each able-bodied citizen, armed and prepared at a moment's notice to defend the republic against external or internal threats. You are already a member of the militia! Your only choice is whether to be ready, willing and able to do your duty.

The militia is a purely defensive entity. It's only capacity is to defend the community against invaders. It lacks the capacity to travel long distances and thus is not a threat to invade a foreign country.

In times of unrest, we will need the militia to prevent a collapse into complete chaos.

Even if the federal government collapses or, worse yet, becomes a rogue tyranny, our federal system provides a framework for survival. We will still have municipalities, counties and states. Militias organized by town, county and state can provide order and defend against any organized threats.

If the Constitution ceases to function entirely, I suggest a quick reversion to the prior governing document, never properly repealed in the first place, the Articles of Confederation.[17] In that regime, much to be preferred in the best of times, each state was largely autonomous but sent representatives to a Congress of the states to resolve certain confederal matters such as defense and interstate commerce.

When will it be time for local militias to swing into action to defend the people from tyranny?

I am on record opposing any illegal or violent tactics against the bellicose kleptocracy on the Potomac. At this point, such tactics merely evidence a failure of the imagination. We can beat these scoundrels with the lethal weapon between our ears. That's the point of this book.

Yet, things are getting dicey and Patriots should understand in advance when we will need to take the fight to a different level. This will always be a judgment call but here are some general guidelines.

---

[17] The Articles required unanimous consent of thirteen *state legislatures* for amendment; the Constitution took effect when nine *state conventions* ratified it. Oops!

A good rule of thumb—when strange men in strange uniforms come into your neighborhood and start abusing innocent civilians, consider that your Paul Revere wakeup call: "The Redcoats are here, the Redcoats are here."

Another good rule. You should probably resist tyranny *before* they knock on your door in the middle of the night and put you into a concentration camp.

Here are some specific criteria for when active resistance to tyranny is called for. It is good to broadcast these guidelines to alert Patriots to act but also to put potential dictators on notice that this or that violation of the Constitution will trigger *immediate and massive resistance*. Let's all be clear on this well in advance.

So, here's my list of illegal and tyrannical acts that justify full and active resistance by Patriots:

1. Mass confiscation of firearms.
2. Mass arrests without probable cause
3. Any crack down on free speech, press or assembly.
4. Martial law (other than during an invasion by a foreign army)
5. Prohibition of homeschooling or private schools.
6. House-to-house searches or permanent roadblocks or checkpoints.

At some point you have to say, enough is enough. **But never fire the first shot.** The Feds have made a career of manipulating their foes into firing the first shot and then claiming the moral high ground.

Any active resistance must be strictly confined within the bounds of just war principles. It must be defensive only, proportional to the attack, and must avoid harming innocent third parties. That's the other side's shtick.

Let me close this admittedly grim chapter with this thought. Everything the liberty movement has been doing for 40 years has been designed to ward off the economic and social collapse of the nation and a lapse into unrest and tyranny. If the political class had only restrained their greedy and power hungry ways for a moment and paid the slightest bit of attention to us, we would not be in the mess we are in.

If civil unrest occurs, 100 percent of the blame will go to those who brought the nation to the present sad state and then piggishly ignored all the warning signs and indeed, *smeared* those who sought peaceful and positive change: the politicians, special interests, plutocrats and their mainstream media flacks and flunkies.

Conclusion

Will this plan to take America back with peaceful and legal direct citizen action succeed? I believe it will if it gets a good start. I believe if it gets started, it will be unstoppable, like an idea whose time has come— *back.*

But this I know for certain. If we do not try to spark a Second American Revolution, we *will* fail and you, your children, and your grandchildren, will never know what it is like to live in the America that was supposed to be. And, with the government always strengthening its stranglehold on the schools, they won't even have a historical memory of it.

George Washington, who led the fight in battle for the American Revolution, and knew a thing or two about adversity, about temporary defeat, about being outnumbered, about being accused of treason, and about being shot at by Redcoats, said, "Perseverance and spirit have done wonders in all ages."

So in closing I urge you to make this pledge:

I pledge allegiance to the principles of the American Revolution, stated by Jefferson, and for which the Minute Men and Washington's Army fought: that government's only purpose is to protect our natural rights to life, liberty, and property; that any government that does "more" than protect our natural rights must thereby violate those same rights and become a tyranny that the people have the right to alter or abolish. I pledge to resist that tyranny by peaceful means if at all possible.

Appendix "A"

Examples of Direct Citizen Action

Below is a list of methods of direct citizen action drawn from a longer list compiled by the Einstein Institute and based on Dr. Gene Sharp's 1973 book, *The Politics of Nonviolent Action, Vol. 2: The Methods of Nonviolent Action.* (Boston: Porter Sargent Publishers, 1973).

- Picketing
- Mock elections
- Displays of flags and symbolic colors
- Wearing of symbols
- "Haunting" officials
- Taunting officials
- Humorous skits and pranks
- Political mourning
- Mock funerals
- Social boycott
- Selective social boycott
- Excommunication
- Student strike
- Consumers' boycott
- Nonconsumption of boycotted goods
- Merchants' "general strike"
- Withdrawal of bank deposits
- Refusal of a government's money
- General strike
- Withholding or withdrawal of allegiance
- Refusal of public support
- Literature and speeches advocating resistance

- Boycott of elections
- Boycott of government employment and positions
- Boycott of government depts., agencies, and other bodies
- Withdrawal from government educational institutions
- Boycott of government-supported organizations
- Reluctant and slow compliance
- Nonobedience in absence of direct supervision
- Selective refusal of assistance by government
- The fast
- Reverse trial
- Guerrilla theater
- Alternative social institutions
- Alternative communication system

Economics in Five Lessons

Power and Market Don't Mix

By James Ostrowski

March 16, 2006

Introduction. The decline of the Western New York economy over the last 45 years is best explained by economics. Only when the people of this area understand the basic economic principles and political dynamics that explain our decline, will they support the policy changes necessary to revive that economy. This essay will outline the five lessons of economics that we believe are most important for understanding our plight and how to get out of it.

The laws of economics cannot be evaded or avoided any more than the laws of physics can be ignored. Human beings are free to engage in any action that is physically possible. Neither physics nor economics says otherwise. People are free to jump out of airplanes without parachutes, and people are free to enact minimum wage laws. We are, however, absolutely *unfree* when it comes to avoiding the consequences of our actions as dictated by physical or economic law. The jumper will be crushed to death by a collision with the ground which unleashes an amount of energy strictly determined by his mass and speed and the density of the ground. The minimum wage law will cause all those perceived by employers to be unable to produce sufficient gross revenue to justify their wages, not to be hired, or, worse, to be fired. It *will* cause unemployment. Our only options with respect to natural laws are to ignore them at our peril or study them so we can adjust our behavior accordingly and be happy.

Here's lesson No. 1:

1.   *All economic resources are scarce.*

The resources we use to produce the goods and services we want are land, labor and capital. We could also add ideas and knowledge as the product of our past labors. All those resources are scarce compared to our virtually unlimited human wants. Our human imagination, which is virtually infinite, can always conjure up new needs and wants when prior needs and wants have been satisfied.

Resources used for one purpose are thereby rendered unavailable for other purposes at the same time. In economics, this is known as *opportunity cost*. *Cost* is not the same as *price*, though they are closely related concepts. The monetary price of a loaf of bread may be two dollars, leading some to think that cost is an objective, calculable thing. That would cheer the hearts of central planners everywhere. On the contrary, cost is purely *subjective*. The cost of that loaf of bread is not two dollars, but the subjectively-felt loss of the good or service we cannot buy because we bought the bread instead.

The point is that cost is not objective, mathematically calculable, or comparable between or among persons. Rather, it is entirely subjective, not subject to mathematical calculation, and not comparable between or among individuals. There is no rational way a politician, central planner or bureaucrat can conclude that the cost of taxing John Doe $100 is *less* than the value of giving John Smith that same money through some government program.

As with many other economic principles and concepts, the concepts of opportunity cost and the subjectivity of value have been entirely ignored by policymakers in Western New York for 45 years. The results of that indifference are readily apparent.

Since all resources are scarce, no economic system can fulfill all needs and wants at the same time. Thus, it is not a fair criticism of any economic system that it fails to do so. Rather, the question is, which system is the best or better than the others at meeting human needs and wants?

Our choices are limited, though this is obscured by the apparent availability of a variety of different economic and political systems. All such systems can be boiled down to whether they use choice or force in allocating scarce resources. They may use force or choice in varying degrees for different purposes, but it is the decision to use choice or force in various amounts which ultimately determines the kind of economic system a given society has.

For example, Tiger Woods possesses a valuable economic resource: the ability to golf better than anyone in the world. Other people desire this service and will pay for it. How do we allocate this scarce resource? Choice or force? We can either let Tiger and those who wish to see him play decide whether he will play, where and for how much, or, we can point a gun at him and make him play and dictate the terms to him.

Which do we do? Surprisingly, we do *both*. We allow Tiger to decide whether or not to play and where and for whom and for how much. We do not force anyone to watch him play or pay him for playing. However, after the golf tournament is over, and money has changed hands, people do go in at gunpoint and make Tiger and the other participants fork over large sums of money by force. If the people who take those profits by force did so without the sanction of the law, we would call them criminals. Since they do it with the sanction of the law, we call them government agents or the taxman.

So, let's call a system based on choice *the market*. Let's call a system based mainly on force, *socialism*. And let's call a mixture of the two pure types of systems, *a mixed economy*. In the United States, we have a mixed economy because we sometimes rely on choice, *the market*, but other times we rely on force, or *socialism*.

For example, the computer industry—hardware, software, and the internet—is relatively unregulated and not heavily subsidized. It is therefore the most dynamic area of the economy featuring an endless supply of new products often less expensive than the ones they replaced. Consumer satisfaction is high. In sharp contrast, the primary and secondary education industry is highly regulated and heavily subsidized. It features a high degree of consumer dissatisfaction. Its products and services change little from year to year while costs increase continually. The main difference between these two industries is that *consumer choice* dominates in computers while *government force* predominates in education.

In summary, since all economic resources are scarce, we must decide whether to allocate them on the basis of force or choice, or some mixture of force and choice.

While lesson number one may seem perfectly obvious to all, its truth is often ignored in political debate. Politicians who propose an endless series of new spending programs to fulfill unmet needs are implicitly denying the truth that economic resources are scarce and that not all human needs and wants can be satisfied.

Whenever you hear a politician propose a new spending program, you are really hearing someone deny that all resources are scarce. They rarely talk about the cost of these new programs, the real costs to real people they know nothing about who will lose their hard-earned dollars and have to give up their personal dreams so that some politician can buy votes with their money.

2. *The market increases wealth by providing incentives to invest in capital.*

Other than by people working longer or harder, the only way wealth can be increased is by investment in land, labor or capital. We invest when we take resources we could consume *now* and use them to increase productivity in the *future*. In an economy based on free choice, there is a strong incentive to invest in capital and labor because the owner can then reap the rewards of increased productivity. No one can come in later when the business is making a profit and force the owner to turn over profits to them.

In the market, all relationships are voluntary and therefore no trade occurs unless both parties expect to benefit. The market is therefore the means by which individuals can pursue their goals in harmony with others.

Entrepreneurs are essential to the proper functioning of the market system. Their role is to perceive needs and wants not yet satisfied in the market. They then gather together the factors of production necessary to provide such needed goods and services, produce them, market them and distribute them to consumers. Shrewd entrepreneurs who make good decisions tend to accumulate more and more capital that allows them to bring to market ever greater numbers and kinds of desirable goods and services. However, the judgment of the market is unforgiving and if they begin to make poor decisions, they will not only fail to earn profits but may lose their entire investment. The market rewards success and punishes failure but today's failures can be tomorrow's successes.

It is because of entrepreneurs that the market is self-correcting. If there are inadequacies in existing goods and services or companies, clever entrepreneurs seeking profits will conjure up other goods and services that better meet those needs or in fact correct defects in existing products. For example, if network newscasts are perceived to be slanted toward one political viewpoint, talk radio entrepreneurs will offer a different product. If talk radio hosts play fast and loose with the facts, blogging entrepreneurs will start websites that track and monitor their shows to keep them in line.

3. *Socialist and mixed economies decrease wealth by reducing incentives to invest in capital.*

In an economy based on force, people will be less likely to invest in the future because of the likelihood that force will be used to siphon off the wealth so produced. Using force to take wealth from some so that it can be invested by others does not increase the total amount of investment. It merely redirects capital from one area of the economy—the market sector—to another area—the socialist sector. Nor is this a zero-sum game since capital is shifted from the productive sector of the economy to the far less productive sector.

The problem of scarce resources cannot be solved by government spending. Government expenditures must be paid for by the opportunities lost to those who have paid the taxes that made those expenditures possible. For example, when the government subsidizes one business with tax money, those funds are thereby unavailable to the taxpayers for investment, savings or expenditures in the market. Those losses are almost never considered or discussed when such corporate welfare schemes are being proposed. It doesn't help that those losses are invisible since they represent projects that do not exist because the government pilfered the necessary funds.

To put it another way, every time government tries to solve a problem by new spending, it creates a new problem by taking resources from people that they had been applying to meeting their most urgent needs and wants.

In deciding whether to use force or choice to allocate resources, we need to consider the issue of *incentives*. The type of system we have will affect the incentives people have to produce or not produce wealth. In a system based on choice, if people wish to improve their economic condition, their incentive will be to produce goods and services that other people will want and will choose to pay for in the market.

In a system based on force, people will generally be motivated to *produce force*, or to be part of organizations that use force to allocate economic resources. That way, they can use that force to direct economic resources to themselves. Conversely, in a system based on force, there will be a disincentive to produce goods and services because you do not have control over their distribution and cannot receive what you perceive to be their full value in any transaction. Rather, the goods and services you produce will tend to be taken from you by force in exchange for little or no compensation. Thus, *economies based on force reduce the incentive of all to produce wealth and increase the incentive to produce force.* Since productive work is not fully rewarded, there is an increased incentive to remain idle, since leisure is not taxed. There will also be thriving black markets as people try to produce goods and services outside the reach of regulatory and tax regimes.

If we look at the peak years of Soviet Communism, a system based almost entirely on brute force, we see that the Soviets maintained an enormous and powerful army, a large and ruthless secret police force, and a huge and horrendous prison system. The Soviets invested in force because force was the coin of the realm.

In democratic mixed economies, there is still a large investment in force. Many people believe that democratic governments don't use force because the people "consent" by participating in elections. This is nonsense. We can see why by asking: what are the people voting *for?* They are voting to get their party into *power* so they can wield the levers of government *force* on their behalf. That's why we have *three million people* in the military or law enforcement. George Washington famously recognized that "government is force." Democratic force is mediated through constitutions, voting, and court decisions, but that doesn't make it any less real. If people don't obey the government's edicts and laws, they will be forced to do so at gunpoint.

If you look hard, you can see the enormous investments that people have made in ensuring access to the levers of force in our mixed economy: hordes of lobbyists and lawyers and pressure groups crowding our capitals and political machines totaling millions of people operating in every county and state and nationally. With government force controlling such a large portion of our economy, we have invested billions of dollars and untold human energies and time to influence the use of that force, resources that in a market economy would be freed up for much more productive pursuits.

What the *entrepreneur* is to the market, the *politician* is to the mixed economy or socialism. Let's compare the two. Both entrepreneurs and politicians purport to be problem-solvers. There is no doubt that entrepreneurs deserve that title. Just think of what Edison, Ford, and Bill Gates have done for the world. In contrast, our most famous politicians are known for presiding over wars. That's a subject beyond our scope today, but let's consider the role of the politician further.

It is hard to think of a politician who got elected in the last 100 years by promising to protect life, liberty and property, which are, after the true purposes of law and government. Rather, they often get elected by promising to take some people's money and give it to others. Greedy voters are taken in by the dream that they will be in the receiving line, not the giving line. Knowing nothing about the people whose money he is seizing, the politician just knows that his use for their money is more urgent than theirs. Opportunity cost is a concept he does not consider. As far as he is concerned, the money he seized grew on a tree. While an entrepreneur must raise his capital by persuading investors to contribute, the politicians just order the taxman to go out and grab the needed funds at gunpoint if necessary.

This approach to problem-solving creates more problems than it solves. It destroys capital, disrupts millions of lives, reduces the incentive to produce and increases the incentive to consume without producing, which impoverishes society and eventually hurts all of us. The politician's grand schemes backfire because of the law of unintended consequences: government interventions into the market often result in the exact opposite of what the politicians intend. Rent control reduces the supply of apartments; urban renewal makes neighborhoods less livable; the minimum wage hurts poor workers and so on. The lesson is never learned however, so one failed program is "rescued" by another, which then fails and is "rescued" by a third in an endless chain of failure extending for decades. While the market is *self-correcting*, problems caused by the government tend to be *self-replicating*.

Note that, unlike entrepreneurs, politicians and bureaucrats do not own the *capital* value of government property. Also, as Murray Rothbard argued, they merely temporarily control the government's *income*. These facts explain much.

- In Buffalo, vast tracts of waterfront property have lain fallow for decades. They are owned by a government agency, the Niagara Frontier Transportation Authority (NFTA). The NFTA's managers had no personal incentive to maximize the capital value of that land.
- Politicians and bureaucrats saddle government with debt to fund spending sprees. They get the immediate benefits without incurring any personal liability for the debts since they don't own the capital value of the enterprise.
- Government systematically fails to invest in infrastructure. Why invest in an asset when you don't own its capital value and you won't be around when it crumbles? For example, it was recently reported that the water pipes in Buffalo are leaking, wasting large quantities of clean water. At the same time, various forms of *income* are fully and generously funded including wages and employee benefits.

In contrast to the harmony seen in market relations, economic relationships in socialist and mixed economies are characterized by a high degree of conflict. Whereas market transactions are voluntary and mutually beneficial, when force is used to compel transactions, the interactions become *unilaterally* beneficial. Indeed, it is precisely because one party does not wish to engage in a given transaction, that they must be compelled to do so. Because large numbers of persons are compelled to participate in various government programs such as government schools, those programs are usually fraught with conflict and dissatisfaction. Taxpayers, parents and students regularly attend meetings to express their dissatisfaction with the goings on in government schools. Similar meetings of protest are unheard of with respect to the computer, software or internet industries.

Why the difference? It's simply because the computer business is based on the free choice of all involved and people can use their freedom of choice to produce and purchase precisely those goods and services they desire, whereas such choice is largely absent in government schools. There, *force* is the predominant mode of decision making—through taxation and coercive laws and regulations. (Most regulations are taxes on non-monetary wealth.) A system based on force necessarily creates conflict as those against whom the force is used accurately perceive themselves as victims of the decision makers or as being exploited by them.

4. *Market prices are the only rational way to allocate resources.*

Market prices are the central nervous system of the economy. The price system is the means by which information about the scarcity of and the demand for resources—which information is scattered throughout the economy and otherwise not possessed by any one person—is encapsulated in one simple number: the price of a good or service. Prices fluctuate as various buyers and sellers make purchases or sales of certain goods and services and resources or abstain from making them. Prices tend toward that level which will insure that supply and demand are in balance. At that price, all those who wish to buy will have a supply of the good or service available. Thus, prices convey information about conditions in the world by means of a simple, easy to grasp number—the price of a good or service.

Economic value is subjective. Only individuals can truly know their values and needs and wants. Individual preferences are ranked ordinally, not cardinally. In other words, "1st, 2nd, 3rd, etc., not 1, 2, 3. That being the case, there is no way to mathematically compare one person's preferences with another's. *Central planners and politicians do not and cannot know them.* However, through freely chosen market transactions, individuals make their values *objectively* known to others, alter supply and demand and affect prices. Prices in turn then reflect the sum total of all human knowledge about the scarcity and value of economic resources. High prices lead us to conserve scarce resources while low prices tell us that the good or service is plentiful and need not be so carefully conserved. Lower-priced resources are then used to create more valuable products and commodities. Without market prices, the process of converting lower-priced goods into more valuable ones would be impossible.

When an economy is run by force, the wishes and values of all people are not considered or even known.

Prices no longer reflect actual scarcities and preferences of people; rather, *they reflect the preferences of those with the power to force their preferences on others.* When force is used to directly control prices, disaster ensues. Prices then no longer reflect the relative scarcity and value of goods and services. Scarce goods priced artificially low will tend to disappear and shortages will inevitably result. When prices are set artificially high, the good or service may be available but there will be a shortage of willing and able buyers. Just as prices allow the free market to rationally and efficiently allocate resources, the general absence of market prices in government "enterprises" and for government property prevents government from doing likewise. For example, the complex Bass Pro project in downtown Buffalo calls for a government entity, the Empire State Development Corporation to take title to the old Memorial Auditorium as a tax dodge. Thus, a government entity, whose managers do not own the capital value of their property, will, over time, have no incentive to determine if a sporting goods store is the highest and best use of the building.

With respect to government programs generally, Murray Rothbard explains:

"[T]here is no way that the government, even if it wanted to, could allocate its services to the most important uses and to the most eager buyers. All buyers, all uses, are artificially kept on the same plane. As a result, the most important uses will be slighted. The government is faced with insuperable allocation problems, which it cannot solve *even to its own satisfaction.* Thus, the government will be confronted with the problem: Should we build a road in Place A or place B? There is no rational way whatever by which it can make this decision. It cannot aid the private consumers of this road in the best way. It can decide only according to the whim of the ruling government official, i.e., only if *government officials* do the "consuming," and not the public. If the government wishes to do what is best for the public, it is faced with an impossible task."[18]

Thus, when the government officials on the newly-created Erie Canal Harbor Development Corporation choose plans for how to spend government money and how to utilize government land on the Buffalo waterfront, they are in effect choosing based on *their personal preferences and values*, not having any possible way of knowing what the public's priorities are. (Asking the public's opinion on a survey or at a public meeting tells us *nothing* about what costs those persons would be willing to pay *out of their own pockets* for the projects they prefer. Thus, such commonly used approaches do not remotely replicate the efficiency of market choices.)

5.   *Taxes will rarely be spent the way you want.*

When you have a dollar in your pocket, you are the absolute master of that dollar. Unless it slips through a hole in your pocket, you *will* spend it on a good or service that you believe will improve your life in some small way. What happens when the taxman reaches into your pocket and takes that dollar from you by force, by threatening you with jail unless you pay up? We often complain about how our tax money is spent, but such complaints really miss the point of taxation. *The point of taxation is to take your funds*

---

[18] Man, Economy and State, p. 820. Online at http://www.mises.org/rothbard/mes/chap12d.asp#9D._F allacy_Government_Business_Basis

because you would not spend them the way the authorities want them spent. They take your money to spend it on programs, projects and policies that differ from your own priorities. If they did not differ, they wouldn't have to tax you.

So, *the essence of taxation is to take your money and spend it on things you oppose.* Once you understand that simple but elusive and painful truth, you will no longer be mystified by the so-called waste of your tax dollars. They may be wasted from your point of view, but they are not wasted from the point of view of those who spend your tax dollars: the bureaucrats and politicians and their infinite list of clients. Just as you will spend your funds on your highest and most urgent needs and wants, they too are now spending *your* tax dollars on *their own* needs and wants. You may moan and groan about the Defense Department paying $1,000 for a toilet seat, but the manufacturer of that toilet seat was laughing all the way to the bank.

In sum, money in your pocket will be spent on your most urgent wants and needs. Once the taxman grabs it, kiss it goodbye. You could spend lots of time and money trying to influence how it is spent by lobbying your legislators and so on. However, you will then be expending further valuable economic resources: your time, energy, and money, in a largely futile effort to recapture your lost control over your own money. You will almost always be wasting your time.

Summary. Economic resources are scarce. They are best allocated by their owners in freely chosen transactions in a free market. That system provides the greatest incentive to invest in the resources—land, labor and capital—needed to produce the various goods and services we call wealth.

Allocating resources based on force will *reduce the total amount of wealth in society and will only benefit a minority who are clever enough to gain control over the levers of power.* In that system, people invest not in wealth but in force so they can confiscate the wealth of others. The market creates wealth. Socialism and our own mixed economy destroy it. The empirical evidence for this is overwhelming. West Germany was far wealthier than East Germany; Hong Kong was and is far wealthier than the rest of China. The most socialist economy on earth—North Korea's—is the poorest in Asia. The United States was far wealthier than the Soviet Union. America's freer economy is far ahead of Mexico's more socialist regime. The more socialist areas of the United States—mainly in the Rust Belt—have been falling behind economically for decades. When Buffalo's economy was market-based, it was world class. As it became more socialized, it steadily declined.

The political ramifications of all this are clear. Government should be reduced to a few minimal functions that the market would have difficulty providing such as courts, police and prisons. Taxes must be kept to an absolute minimum and replaced by user fees wherever possible. Political power should be decentralized so that governments compete with each other in keeping taxes low and so that people can easily vote with their feet if their local governments become oppressive.

That is the Free Buffalo plan[19], our best hope for reversing our 45-year-long decline and making Buffalo great and good again.

---

[19] Freebuffalo.org/mission_statement.htm.

Bibliography/Recommended Readings for Appendix "B"

This essay is written from what is called the Austro-libertarian point of view. (No originality as to the basic ideas and principles is claimed.) That perspective combines insights from the Austrian School of Economics with libertarian political analysis. The following books would be helpful to those wishing to pursue these lines of thought in greater detail. Free Buffalo does not necessarily endorse all the views expressed in these works.

Bastiat, Frédérick, "The Law," in *Selected Essays on Political Economy*, George B. de Huszar, ed. (Irvington-on-Hudson, N.Y.: Foundation for Economic Education, 1995), p. 52.

Callahan, Gene, *Economics for Real People, An Introduction to the Austrian School* (Auburn, AL: Mises Institute, 2002)

Henry Hazlitt, *Economics in One Lesson* (Fiftieth Anniversary Edition, San Francisco: Fox & Wilkes, 1996)

Higgs, Robert, *Crisis and Leviathan: Critical Episodes in the Growth of Government* (New York: Oxford University Press, 1987)

Hoppe, Hans-Hermann, *Democracy: the God That Failed* (New Brunswick, NJ: Transaction Publishers, 2002)

Locke, John, The Second Treatise of Civil Government (1690)

Mises, Ludwig von, *Human Action: The Scholar's Edition* (Auburn, AL: Mises Institute, 1998 [1949])

http://www.mises.org/humanaction.asp

Ostrowski, James, *Political Class Dismissed* (Buffalo, N.Y.: Cazenovia Books, 2004)

Reisman, George. *Capitalism: A Treatise on Economic.* (Jameson Books, 1998)
http://www.capitalism.net/Capitalism/CAPITALISM%20Internet.pdf

Rockwell, Llewellyn H., *Speaking of Liberty* (Auburn, AL: Mises Institute, 2003)

Rothbard, Murray N.,

————*For a New Liberty,* (Collier Books: New York, rev. ed. 1978)
http://www.mises.org/rothbard/newliberty.asp
————Man, Economy, and State (Auburn, AL: Mises Institute, 1993 [1962]).
http://mises.org/rothbard/mes.asp

————*Power and Market: Government and the Economy* (Kansas City: Sheed Andrews and McMeel, 1970)

Websites

The most comprehensive source for information about the Austro-libertarian tradition is Mises.org, the website of the Ludwig von Mises Institute.

Free Buffalo's philosophy and plan contain elements drawn from populism, libertarianism, and New England-style town meeting democracy. In a word: *Jeffersonian.* To support Free Buffalo's efforts to restore Western New York's economy, visit FreeNewYork.org.

Bibliography and Resources

FreeStateProject.org (voting with your feet)

TenthAmendmentCenter.com (state sovereignty)

PoliticalClassDismissed.com (political activism)

FreetheChildren.US
(pull your kids of out of government school)

SchoolandState.org (school choice)

ExodusMandateProject.org
(encourages Christian families to leave government schools)

Books

de la Boétie, Étienne *The Politics of Obedience: The Discourse of Voluntary Servitude* (1553)

Ostrowski, James, *Government Schools Are Bad for Your Kids: What You Need to Know* (Buffalo, NY: Cazenovia Books, 2009)

Rothbard, Murray, *For a New Liberty* (Collier Books: New York, rev. ed. 1978)

Sharp, Gene, *Politics of Nonviolent Action* (3 vols.) (Boston: Porter Sargent, 1973)

Sun Tzu, *The Art of War* (6th century BC)

About the Author

James Ostrowski is a trial and appellate lawyer and libertarian writer from Buffalo, New York. He graduated from St. Joseph's Collegiate Institute in 1975 and obtained a degree in philosophy from the State University of New York at Buffalo in 1980 and a law degree from Brooklyn Law School in 1983.

He served as vice-chairman of the law reform committee of the New York County Lawyers Association (1986-88) and wrote two widely quoted reports critical of the law enforcement approach to the drug problem. *New York Newsday* described his report on drug-related AIDS as "superb." He has written a number of scholarly articles on the law on subjects ranging from drug policy to the commerce clause of the Constitution. He has written several bar association reports and given continuing legal education lectures on *habeas corpus*, lawsuits against government officials and jury nullification.

His articles have appeared in the *Wall Street Journal, Buffalo News, Cleveland Plain Dealer* and *Legislative Gazette*. His policy studies have been published by the Hoover Institution, the Ludwig von Mises Institute and the Cato Institute. He taught a course in the Constitution at Canisius College in Buffalo and has been a guest lecturer at the University at Buffalo Medical School.

Presently he is an Adjunct Scholar at the Ludwig von Mises Institute and columnist for LewRockwell.com. He is editor of the libertarian blog, PoliticalClassDismissed.com and Founder and President of the Jeffersonian think tank, Free New York, Inc.

He is the author of *Political Class Dismissed* (2004) and *Government Schools Are Bad for Your Kids* (2009).

Made in the USA
Lexington, KY
13 June 2010